MUSHROOMS

MILLICENT E. SELSAM

MUSHROOMS

PHOTOGRAPHS BY
JEROME WEXLER

William Morrow and Company, Inc.
New York

For Daniel Howard Selsam

PHOTO CREDITS All photographs are by Jerome Wexler with the exception of the following: p. 14, Neg. No. 323356, Courtesy Department Library Services, American Museum of Natural History; p. 17, The Bettmann Archive; p. 16, The Metropolitan Museum of Art, The Elisha Whittlesey Collection, The ElishaFund, 1944 (44.7.34); pp. 12-13, 30, U.S. Department of Agriculture. Permission is gratefully acknowledged.

Printed in the United States of America.

1 2 3 4 5 6 7 8 9 10

Library of Congress Cataloging-in-Publication Data

Selsam, Millicent Ellis, 1912–   Mushrooms.
    Includes index. Summary: Discusses the history, structure, and types of mushrooms and describes how one variety is grown.
    1. Mushrooms—Juvenile literature.   2. Mushroom culture—Juvenile literature.   [1. Mushrooms]
I. Wexler, Jerome, ill.   II. Title.   QK617.S379   1986   589.2'223   85-18953
ISBN 0-688-06248-2
ISBN 0-688-06249-0 (lib. bdg.)

BY MILLICENT E. SELSAM
AND JEROME WEXLER

The Amazing Dandelion
Catnip
Cotton
Eat the Fruit, Plant the Seed
Mimosa, The Sensitive Plant
Plants We Eat, *Newly Revised Edition*
Popcorn

The author wishes to thank the growers of Franklin Mushroom Farms, North Franklin, Connecticut, for their kind help with the commercial growing section of this book.

She would also like to thank John C. Cooke, Associate Professor of Biology at The University of Connecticut, Groton, for his help in identifying the mushrooms on pages 41–45 of the book.

CONTENTS

AUTHOR'S NOTE

Although there are many different species of mushrooms, the one described in this book is the kind you are likely to buy at the market. Its scientific name is *Agaricus bisporus*.

1
HISTORY

There is something mysterious and ghostlike about a plant that is not green, has no leaves or roots, and springs up suddenly after rainstorms. It is no wonder, then, that for thousands of years people puzzled over mushrooms and made up stories about them: Were they formed by lightning that hit the ground? Did toads sit on these little plants that looked like stools? Did fairies dance on the caps of mushrooms or use them as umbrellas?

A mushroom "fairy ring."

12

Certain kinds of mushrooms form circles as they grow out in all directions from the center. People called them "fairy rings" because the circles of mushrooms appeared so suddenly they seemed like magic.

Some types of mushrooms contained chemicals that made people dance wildly and have strange visions and dreams. This made people think that mushrooms were enchanted.

In Mexico and Central America, primitive people carved stone sculptures known as mushroom stones. They may have been used in religious ceremonies. Most of these stones were made between 200 B.C. and 300 A.D., but some of them were carved as long ago as 2000 B.C.

A PRIMITIVE MUSHROOM STONE.

On the other side of the world there are records of mushrooms in Egyptian tombs. A painting of a mushroom has recently been discovered on a mural from the tomb of Pharoah Amenemhep that was done around 1450 B.C.

Ancient Greeks valued mushrooms as food; and a Greek doctor names Hippocrates, who was born in 460 B.C., wrote about using mushrooms as medicine. Later, Theophrastus, a Greek physician (371–287 B.C.) wrote a book on plants and proclaimed that mushrooms belonged to the plant world.

Romans also knew about mushrooms. A Roman soldier and scholar, Pliny the Elder, who lived during the first century A.D., added to the body of information about these plants. He noted that mushrooms grew in the ground, especially after a rainstorm. He also gave guidelines for telling poisonous from edible mushrooms.

Romans were so fond of eating this plant that specially trained mushroom collectors were sent out to find and bring back those that could safely be eaten.

After the decline of the Roman Empire, there was little mention of mushrooms for a long while. But during the Middle Ages, in the sixteenth and seventeenth centuries, botanical books called "herbals" were written. In them the use of plants as food and medicine were described. Mushrooms often appeared in them.

A PAGE FROM A SIXTEENTH-CENTURY HERBAL.

As time passed, a great deal of knowledge about mushrooms was accumulated, and careful observation took the place of superstition.

By the nineteenth century, the French were growing mushrooms in caves around Paris. The English were also growing these plants and shipping them to other countries. In the last hundred years, mushroom houses with controlled growing conditions were developed. This made it possible to grow mushrooms without troublesome insects or molds destroying the crops.

MUSHROOM CAVES AROUND PARIS.

2

THE
PLANT

Mushrooms seem to appear suddenly, but that is because they have been developing for awhile under the ground or inside the bark of a tree. The underground parts look like mats of cottony threads. The part we know as a mushroom grows from these underground "threads."

18

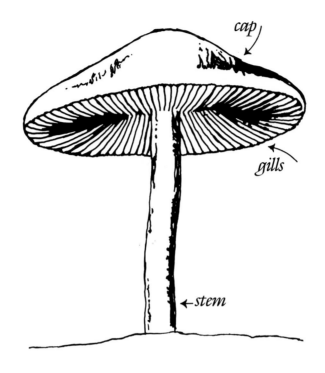

cap

gills

←stem

The mushroom is a fungus, the kind of plant that is not green and that feeds on live or decaying plant material around it.

The most noticeable part of a mushroom is the *cap*. The shape of it helps to tell different kinds of mushrooms apart. On the underside of the cap are *gills*, which look like the partly open leaves of a book.

The gills bear *spores*. A spore, like a seed, will grow into a new plant when it falls on a moist place. The spore sends out a rootlike thread called *hypha*. Several of these hyphae crisscrossed together is called the *mycelium*. The commercial growers' term for it is *spawn*.

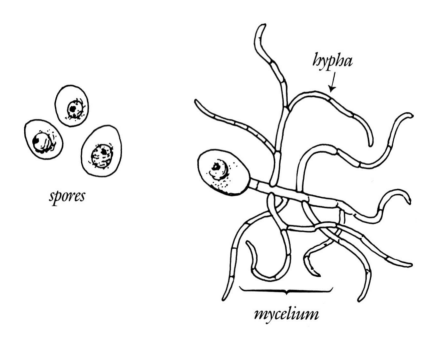

spores

hypha

mycelium

Here is a close-up view of the mycelium.

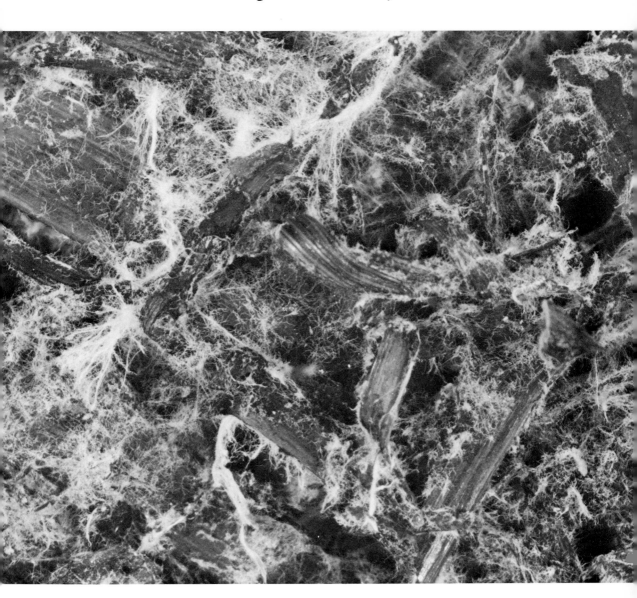

At some point, small white bumps begin to develop on the mycelium. These bumps will develop into the part of the plant we know as a mushroom. In this photograph, one mushroom has pushed its way up through the mycelium. Around it are smaller, "button" mushrooms that are still growing. They are attached to the mycelium.

The mushroom grows bigger.

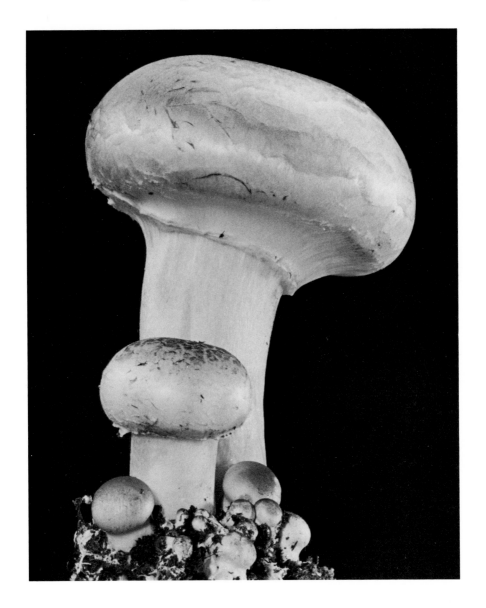

As it grows, the cap begins to open up like an umbrella. The *veil,* the delicate membrane that covers the under part of the cap, is breaking.

Here the veil has broken away and you can see the gills clearly.

The gills darken as the spores they bear mature. When the spores are fully developed, they fall out of the cap and onto the ground. A typical mushroom produces about a million spores a minute over a period of a few days.

Spores are tiny and hard to see without a magnifying glass. But you can see lots of them together, if you make a spore print.

To make one, use a ripe, store-bought mushroom—one where the cap has opened and the gills are visible. Cut off the stem of the mushroom just below the cap. Lay the cap, with the gills facing down, on a piece of white paper. Cover the mushroom cap with a glass to keep the spores from blowing away.

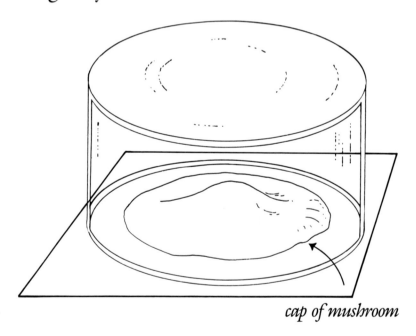

cap of mushroom

The next day you should see a print like this:

3

GROWING MUSHROOMS

The mushrooms you buy in the store are grown on special mushroom farms. They are grown on a certain kind of soil called *compost*, which consists of decayed organic matter. The organic matter can be horse stable bedding, or man-made compost consisting of a mixture of corncobs, straw, and hay. Natural fertilizers such as cottonseed, meal, and soybean oil are usually added.

When the stable bedding or corncob mixture is received at a mushroom farm, it is stored in large heaps that look like haystacks.

The heaps are kept wet.

After a few days, the piles are broken up and wet again. This process is repeated every two days for five to six days.

The compost is then carried into the mushroom house.

Long trays are filled with the compost to a depth
of ten inches.

The compost is wet once more.

The trays are wheeled into special rooms in which the temperature is raised to between 140° and 150° Fahrenheit (60°–66° Celsius). Keeping the room at this high temperature kills insects, microscopic molds, and unwanted bacteria. The process is called *pasteurization*. After four to six days, the temperature is brought down gradually to between 75° and 80° Fahrenheit (21°–26° Celsius).

The compost is now ready for spawn, which is a pure culture of the cottony white threads of mycelium.

The mycelium used by mushroom growers is from a mushroom with the scientific name *Agaricus bisporus*. Spores of this mushroom are grown on nutrient jelly in sterile conditions in a laboratory. When the delicate white threads of hyphae emerge from these spores, they are transplanted into flasks containing sterilized cereal seeds. The threads soon penetrate the seeds.

It is these seeds that are sold as spawn.

Mushroom growers buy this spawn and mix it into the compost. After a few weeks, the spawn spreads throughout the compost.

SPAWN.

The compost is now covered with a mixture of crushed stone and peat called *casing*. The casing helps the mycelium send up fruiting bodies.

Two weeks after the casing is applied, the mushrooms start to appear. Each week there is a sudden new outbreak of mushrooms, called a *flush*.

Here at last are the mushrooms you recognize, although the main part of the mushroom is the mycelium under the surface.

37

The mushrooms are picked just before the cap
expands to expose the gills.

The mushrooms are sorted according to size and packed in cartons. Then they are sold to fruit and vegetable markets, canneries, and soup makers.

4
DIFFERENT KINDS OF MUSHROOMS

Here are two mushrooms coming through the ground. They look very much alike. One is poisonous. It is called "the destroying angel." The other can be eaten without harm.

40

41

This is just one example of how easily edible mushrooms can be confused with poisonous ones, and shows why only experts should collect mushrooms in the wild.

There are plenty of old wives' tales about the way to tell a poisonous from an edible mushroom. For example, people used to believe that the mushroom is poisonous if a silver coil becomes black when placed in the pot where mushrooms are cooking; the color of the cap tells the poisonous and edible types apart; the odor of the mushroom distinguishes them; mushrooms are safe if a dog or cat can eat them without harm; or that cooking the mushroom kills the poison.

Not one of these is a safe test.

Only careful study over a period of time can make you a mushroom specialist.

This book is about one common type of mushroom. But there are thousands of different kinds that grow wild, and they come in many shapes.

Most of them look like umbrellas or parasols.
Some look like tiny tables.

Some may resemble turkey tails, or they can look like sponges.

Others look like little shelves.
They may even look like balls.

Even if you never eat a wild mushroom, you can have fun taking walks in the woods and noticing the many varieties.

You can find them on forest floors, tree stumps or logs, and as parasites on trees. Many are beautiful to look at. Just remember, they may contain strong chemicals that are poisonous. Do not eat any of them unless you are with a mushroom expert who can assure you they are safe.

INDEX

About the Author

MILLICENT E. SELSAM's career has been closely connected with biology and botany. She majored in biology and was graduated magna cum laude with a B.A. degree from Brooklyn College. At Columbia she received her M.A. and M.Ph. in the Department of Botany. After teaching biology for ten years in the New York City high schools, she devoted herself to writing. The author of more than one hundred science books for children, Ms. Selsam has received the Eva L. Gordon Award of the American Nature Study Society, the Thomas Alva Edison Award, two Boys Club of America awards, and the nonfiction award for the Total Body of Creative Writing given by the Washington Children's Book Guild in 1978. In addition, she is a fellow of the American Association for the Advancement of Science.

At present, Ms. Selsam lives in New York City and spends her summers on Fire Island, New York.

About the Photographer

JEROME WEXLER was born in New York City, where he attended Pratt Institute. Later he studied at the University of Connecticut. His interest in photography started when he was in the ninth grade. After service in World War II, he worked for the State Department in Europe as a photographer. Returning to the United States, he specialized in photographing advanced farming techniques, and the pictures he made have been published throughout the world. Since then he has illustrated more than thirty children's books with his photographs of plants, animals, and insects.

Mr. Wexler lives in Madison, Connecticut.

48